# Come to Me

## Sonia Kinning

Copyright © 2019 Sonia Kinning
ISBN: 978-1-9997955-5-9

All rights reserved.
No part of this publication may be reproduced, stored in a retrieval system, or transmitted in any form or by any means, electronic, mechanical, photocopying or otherwise, without prior written consent of the publisher except as provided by under United Kingdom copyright law. Short extracts may be used for review purposes with credits given.

All Scriptures quoted are taken from New King James Version, except where stated.
Scripture taken from the New King James Version®. Copyright © 1982 by Thomas Nelson. Used by permission. All rights reserved.

Published by
Maurice Wylie Media
Bethel Media House
Tobermore
Magherafelt,
Northern Ireland
BT45 5SG (UK)

Publisher's note: Throughout this book we honour God by capitalizing Godhead pronouns. The name satan and related names are not capitalized. We choose not to acknowledge him, even to the point of violating grammatical rules.

www.MauriceWylieMedia.com

PLACING MINISTRY ONTO PAPER
Create | Brand | Establish

# Dedication

This book is dedicated to my mum, Sandra, and stepdad, Leslie, for all their support and encouragement in writing my first book.

# Acknowledgments

I thank Pastor Sharon Perry for submitting the Foreword, Pastor Ronnie McCreanor for his endorsement, and both of them for taking the time out of their busy schedules to read each poem.

To my loved ones and friends for their great encouragement to write *"Come To Me"*, helping me believe it could happen.

For all the opportunities I have had to share at different church gatherings and the encouragement I received from each of them.

To all who helped to bring this book about...thank you.

# Endorsement

Sonia's poems are inspired by the Holy Spirit and God's Word. You will be encouraged, enlightened, and elated as you read the poems and realise that the God of creation is by your side and on your side, enabling you to be more than a conqueror.

Pastor Ronnie McCreanor
Jordanstown Christian Centre, Newtownabbey, Northern Ireland

I highly recommend you take the time and read these wonderful pieces of art.

Sonia's work is penned with a depth that will touch your spirit and are filled with messages that will speak to everyone who reads them."

Aaron V. Graham
International Christian Songwriter/Recording Artist

# Contents

| | |
|---|---|
| Introduction | 13 |
| The Shut Door | 15 |
| My Beloved | 19 |
| Seek Me Out | 23 |
| Come to Me on the Waters | 27 |
| The Battle | 32 |
| The Valley | 36 |
| I'm Just Up Ahead of You | 41 |
| I see you | 45 |
| Heaven | 49 |
| Hell | 53 |
| I know you | 57 |
| I've Been There | 62 |
| Jesus | 67 |
| The Rescuer Has Come | 71 |
| The Refiner's Fire | 75 |
| Come Away with Me | 79 |
| You're So Beautiful to Me | 83 |
| In the Shadows | 87 |
| Come Soar | 91 |
| Never Alone | 95 |

'Come to Me,
all you who labor and are heavy laden,
and I will give you rest.'


Matthew 11:28

# Foreword

Our heavenly Father has taught us through His Word—which He ordained to be written down for each generation to read and re-read—that words carry power; they are containers of death and life. In today's society, driven by social media, words have been replaced by emojis and reduced to abbreviations unrecognizable to some of us. The written Word has been devalued in many areas of life and so it is encouraging to hear of a young woman passionate about writing and doubly passionate about exalting Jesus in the midst of her generation.

Shortly after Sonia asked me to write this Foreword, she handed me an envelope containing a hand-written collection of the poems that are now printed in this book. The means of presentation emphasized to me the very personal and passionate nature of each line, the thoughts of Sonia's heart poured out through ink onto paper. As you read, you will sense not just the depth of personal experience but a prophetic element that brings much needed edification, exhortation, and comfort in the midst of life's universal challenges.

This is a book of modern-day psalms written by a modern-day psalmist. Sonia encompasses, like David of old, the ups and downs of life, which are common to all—but she also reassures the reader that *"The Rescuer Has Come."* You can be left in no doubt that Sonia knows her beloved Jesus intimately as she displays His banner over her life, encouraging others to seek Him out, the victorious and conquering Light *"In The Shadows."*

Sonia has had first-hand experience of *"The Shut Door,"* but I believe that God has now opened an effectual door before her. In the writing of this book, I pray she will see the way open before her and step into her destiny and all God has in store. I pray that every reader too "will see His wisdom" as doors have closed—and trust Daddy God to direct your steps, knowing "His thoughts for peace, hope, and a future still stand."

God's richest blessing,

Sharon Perry, Senior Pastor
Abundant Grace

Dublin and Belfast, Ireland

# Introduction

My aim in writing Come to Me is to comfort and give great hope to those in need. I pray as people read through these pages that they will find a poem that will touch and comfort them with where they are in life. The Lord Jesus reassures us, time and time again, that He will never leave us nor forsake us, He is always with us (Deuteronomy 31:6).

Life has many different stresses and problems. This book has been an amazing opportunity for me to reach out through these pages to comfort, encourage, and give you hope that Jesus watches over you and He does hear your prayers.

He is our great help in time of need. I want *Come To Me* to be raw and real to readers, to reassure them that there is always hope, there is joy for mourning.

No matter what you're going through, the Lord Jesus will make a way through. You're not alone—Jesus is eternally faithful.

# The Shut Door
## Isaiah 55:8-9

A turn of a key, the lock engages;
secured by the Master's hand.
A shut door to a vision, a dream,
and all that had been planned.
Many unanswered questions,
that only the Lord can meet
As you wrestle with feelings of frustration,
loss and defeat.

Sorrowful tears from heartache,
that just constantly flow,
As you now give your plans back,
step away and let them go.
"My ways are not your ways",
trust Me, though you can't see;
In quietness and confidence,
will be your strength in Me.

## Come to Me

*Informed and instructed,
do not look back anymore,
Do not fret or be concerned over the closing,
of the shut door.
Man's hearts plan his way,
but God shall direct his step,
As you face up to the reality
of your desires unmet.*

*A lamp visibly illuminates
the journey you will take
As you're led from the shut door,
you must now leave and forsake.
His thoughts for peace, a hope,
and a future still stand
Trust in Him completely,
though you can't trace His hand.*

*As He opens the way before you,
soon you will see
The reason He commanded you,
to leave the door be.
As you step into your destiny of what
He has in store,
Now you see His wisdom of why
He closed the shut door.*

# My Beloved
## 1 John 3:1

*I pour My love within you,
every moment of every day;
I am love's greatest expression,
to you, in every way.
I'm forever compassionate towards you,
nothing else compares;
I delight in showing you
how much your Abba Father cares.*

*My love's immensely overwhelming,
you're secure in who I am;
I've an inscription of your name,
tattooed across My palm.
My heart yearns and longs for you,
I'm wanting you to know,
I'm acquainted with all your ways
and will never let you go.*

## Come to Me

*Beloved, never doubt My love for you,*
*I'm always by your side.*
*My love never changes, in your weakness,*
*you've no need to hide.*
*I'm jealous for your affections,*
*I watch you all day long.*
*My love covers all your sin,*
*it doesn't waver when you're wrong.*

*I have placed Myself within you,*
*for all the world to see;*
*My banner over you displayed,*
*to show what you mean to Me.*
*Unconditional and enduring love,*
*perfect in all its ways,*
*How gracefully you are loved,*
*by the Ancient of Days.*

My beloved, My beautiful creation,
I'm dwelling within your heart;
All of Me I give to you, in you,
I gently impart.
I'm whispering I love you,
can you hear Me gently say,
As I pour My love upon you
each and every day.

Adored and tenderly cherished,
is how I feel for you;
I'm unchanging, completely steadfast
and utterly, utterly true.
How I love you My beloved,
I long for you to know,
Where life's journey takes you,
My footprints beside you will go.

# Seek Me Out
## Psalm 42:1

As the deer pants for the waters,
desperately come, seek Me out;
I'm an abundance of many rivers,
not a dry and thirsty drought.
I invite you; will you search for Me,
search throughout the land?
There's no one like Me, in My own
authority, alone in Myself I stand.

Seek Me and you'll find Me,
when you search with all your heart.
Strive after, diligently search
and set yourself apart;
Come and earnestly seek,
step away from all you know.
Hunt Me down, pursue Me,
let the world pass, let it go.

## Come to Me

Willingly I urge you,
look for Me and do not back down;
I am everywhere, keep looking,
I'm so close, I'm all around.
I'm not hiding from you,
come deeper and you will surely see
There's so much more to learn,
more to know about Me.

Eagerly come and hunger,
I am your greatest reward,
Run after and thirst for Me,
come and seek out your Lord.
I will completely satisfy;
earnestly seek and you will see
I'm waiting for you to discover—come,
press deeper into Me.

*So, follow after My leading,*
*you will see Me up ahead;*
*Track Me down, I'm easily found,*
*come feed from the Living Bread.*
*Yes! Seek Me and you'll find*
*I'm everything you need;*
*You cannot do without Me*
*and with Me can you succeed.*

# Come to Me on the Waters
## Isaiah 43:2

I watch the great waters,
come crashing against the stern;
I have things I long to teach you,
things of wisdom to learn.
I'm standing waiting for you,
upon this great raging sea,
Look carefully out among the waves,
that figure you see is Me.

I've come for you;
My invisible power will keep you afloat.
I'm challenging you from this vessel,
will you trust Me and leave this boat?
Stand now and get ready,
keep looking out ahead.
You asked to go deeper,
I'm now answering what you prayed.

## Come to Me

I challenge you now to climb over
and step upon this sea.
Come, I'm within reaching distance,
come My child to Me.
Do not be fearful,
look completely My way;
Leave this vessel,
I'm urging you not to stay.

Do not hesitate,
feel the waters softly below your feet.
I'm calling on this great sea,
I've prepared for us to meet.
I offer you this challenge, come deeper,
I Am so much more;
Step away from this vessel,
as it now heads back to shore.

*Now come to Me,
come, come closer still.
I don't want you in your comfort zone,
for you, it's not My will.
Trust Me!
Yes, keep walking within this swelling tide;
I'll be your lighthouse shining,
your eternal glowing guide.*

*These waters will not overwhelm you,
I won't let you down;
My special beloved child,
I will not let you drown.
Our intimacy I cherish, come to Me, you're almost there;
I've been holding you up
and you've been so unaware.*

_Come to Me_

The winds are howling,
but here beside Me, you stand;
I control these mighty oceans
by the lifting of My hand.
These great roaring seas,
know exactly who I Am;
Watch carefully as I whisper seas be still,
seas be calm.

# The Battle
## 1 Samuel 17:47

*I see your conflict raging,*
*this battle you do not need to face;*
*I have raised up My standard,*
*I will fight in your place.*
*You have no need to worry,*
*your victory won't be long;*
*My armies are marching forward*
*and their Leader is mighty strong.*

*I have dressed you in My armour,*
*on you for a divine display;*
*When demons see your protection,*
*they'll bow down then flee away.*
*Stand firm forever knowing,*
*I'm conquering for you ahead;*
*Holding up My banner,*
*I've all power to raise the dead.*

# The Battle

Your enemy pushes at My defences,
but I mock his feeble way;
Just the mention of My Glory,
is all I need to say.
You see in this battle,
I know exactly what to do;
I'm bringing My heavenly resources,
especially equipped for you.

I'm showing off My Glory,
you will feel Me passing by;
Satan will never defeat you,
but determined he continues to try.
I watch the powers of darkness,
as they make their way to you;
I'm laughing at their confusion,
knowing it's Me you belong to.

## Come to Me

All heaven's troops are advancing,
throughout the atmosphere;
Your enemies now tremble,
Your Great I Am is here.
As I'm fighting in this battle,
legions of angels by My side,
The demons look in wonder
and fearfully try to hide.

All satan's powers are broken,
as they get a better view;
When they see the precious Blood,
I have covered over you.
I'm shielding you from their arrows,
as the enemy takes his aim;
But none of these will harm you,
your protection, is in My Name.

# The Valley
## Psalm 23:4

Gently Jesus beckons, come child,
take My hand;
Lovingly He encourages my feet,
upon the parched land.
I look to the mountains,
they're so endlessly steep.
My steps feel so unsteady,
I feel fearful, I feel so weak.

The earth feels so dry,
as my tears soak into the ground.
Searching for relief,
in my desperation I look around;
As the valley disappears into the distance,
as I look ahead,
Look to Me completely,
are the words that You said.

*Jesus, You promised You would lead me
as I walk through;
I've nothing to fear,
because You said keep trusting in You.
How many more steps,
will I possibly have to take
Before You walk me from this valley,
a way out for me You'll make.*

*Clifftops hover over me,
the sunlight almost blocked out
Shadows close in around me,
but Your love I'll never doubt.
Goodness and mercy,
dwell close by my side
I will walk through this valley,
there's no reason to fear or hide.*

## Come to Me

There's no life in this deadness,
as I keep my gaze upon You,
Knowing that You're with me,
Jesus, You know exactly what to do.
You're perfecting me in this wilderness,
knowing it'll make me strong,
Encouraging me in this deadness,
my deliverance won't be long.

Dry bones lie scattered,
along time they've been here,
As you whisper, this way My child,
my pathway becomes clear.
You comfort and reassure me
as we make this tiresome trek,
Promising me complete recovery,
nothing with You I'll lack.

*The Valley*

*The valley now opens before me,
into a well-watered plain,
Streams of rivers now flowing,
I rejoice and praise Your Name.
Your arm securely around me,
my refuge is completely in You;
Making me more like You,
Jesus, that's exactly what You wanted to do.*

# I'm Just Up Ahead of You
## Romans 12:2

*I'm just up ahead of you,
in your future that I have planned;
Though at times you be confused,
I will help you to understand.
You see, I'm watering your seeds of faith,
that so patiently you have sown;
I'm looking to you smiling,
all for My Glory you have grown.*

*I'm preparing your beauty for ashes,
for all the times you've honoured Me.
The devouring locusts I've now blown
away, My abundance you'll shortly see.
I'm gently handling your heart's desire,
a little time now to go.
I've your future all organised, look,
My goodness is beginning to show.*

## Come to Me

*I'm just up ahead arranging,
as I put everything into its place;
I've answered your prayers already,
My abundance of good things you'll taste.
Divinely I'm intervening,
as My favour is released from My hand;
I'm now moving all those obstacles—your
mountains move at My command.*

*Oh! Just wait and see what
I'm going to do,
My abundance of promises is completely true.
I'm handling those impossibilities,
the ones you see no way through.
So joyful at what you're going to see,
I've created a way forward for you.*

You're now ready for what
I've prepared for you,
you'll be in awe at what's up ahead.
You're going to reap My abundance of joy,
in place of sorrow instead.
I've made everything work together,
as I promised that I would;
I'm pouring out all My blessings,
over you, for your good.

I'm just up ahead of you,
I've placed a guiding lamp at your feet.
Times are set and divine connections made,
with the people I want you to meet.
I've created doors where there are no doors,
that stay open as long as I say.
You see, your future knows who I Am,
I'm your Father, who shows you His way.

# I see you
## Deuteronomy 31:8

I have all your problems resting in My hand;
My child, do not agonize to work them out,
they're under My command.
I see what you're thinking,
as you wrestle with what to do;
Stop fretting My child,
I've it already sorted out for you.

I can see that smile that hides your pain;
I'm always aware when
you're crying out My Name.
Yes! You don't know what to do,
But it's all about My timing,
My heart, My way for you.

## Come to Me

I see you in turmoil as you reach for the phone;
Please know I'm holding you together,
you're not suffering this alone.
I see all those pressures
that battle to weigh you down;
Remember child, I'm your King,
the one who wears the crown.

I see you awake, each sleepless night;
I walk with you, as you pace the floor,
deciding what is right.
I do see that look that fills your eye,
The one that holds tears as you try not to cry.

*I see you*

*My dear one,
I see everything that makes you sigh.
I'm working in your pain,
you've no need to worry why.
I Am your great God Almighty,
look completely to Me.
Do not look to the left or right,
My miracles you are going to see.*

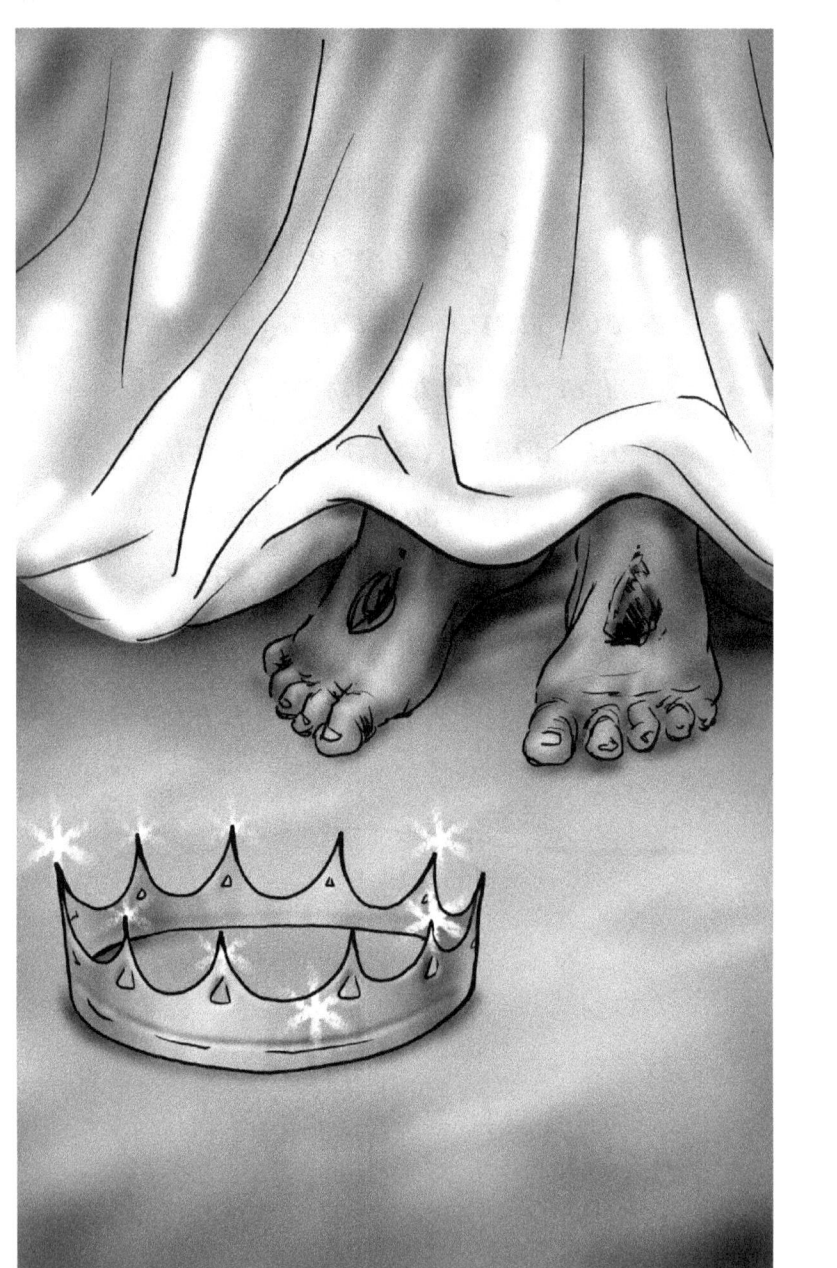

# Heaven
## Revelation 4

The gates of splendour are open,
they shine from the purest gold.
Here, life goes on forever, no ending,
so the story is told.
The light that shines the brightest
is from our Majestic King,
As nonstop praise and worship
—all hail the Lamb, we'll sing.

No tears or sadness lives here,
it will all just disappear;
Endless laughing and celebrations
are all we'll ever hear.
Here comes the King of Glory
as we look to Him amazed;
Our minds will have forgotten,
our pain will have all been erased.

## Come to Me

A paradise prepared for His children,
the redeemed whom He set free;
We'll bask in His love and glory,
to Him all praises shall be.
The great banquet tables are ready,
a feast will soon take place;
We'll take off our crowns of beauty
and look into His beautiful face.

The streets of diamonds and gemstones,
all made by the Master's hand,
As the crystal-clear river flows,
throughout our heavenly land.
The ticking clock doesn't exist here,
eternity is all we'll know,
As we fall on our knees and worship,
King Jesus who loves us so.

The darkest night will never arrive here,
the heavens will always shine;
As eternity continues forever,
I am His and He is mine.
Jesus now stands before us,
the radiance from His face we'll see;
As He looks to each of His children, saying,
"My precious ones, you belong to Me!"

The trumpets now echo in triumph,
as each child He welcomes home;
Forever we'll be with Jesus,
as we gather around His throne.
Our loved ones hurry to meet us,
in our joy we'll hear our name
As Jesus joyfully calls us, together,
forever we'll reign.

# Hell
### Matthew 25:41

Piercing screams of agony,
where can this be?
A lake of agonizing torment,
where captured souls will never flee.
Reaching out into the darkness,
desperately wanting to die;
Relentlessly searching a way out,
eternity in hell they cry.

Completely terrorised and forsaken,
forever alone in their pain;
Rejected by the Saviour,
for no repentance of their sin or shame.
Begging and pleading for His mercy,
but now it's far too late;
The cost of rejecting His salvation,
and the accepting of satan's bait.

*Come to Me*

Wails of absolute horror,
humankind wasn't made for this place;
Still they call for the Master,
but no longer will He plead their case.
Forever the lake surrounds them,
this is where they'll stay;
Eternal punishment in hell,
for rejecting "The Truth and The Way".

The raging flames engulf them,
a lake that has no end;
Desperately crying for their freedom,
a prison they cannot apprehend.
Oh the unbelievable torment
that the godless souls must bear;
Left in agony forever,
there's no one to comfort them there.

## Hell

There's no ending to their suffering,
this is what will always be;
No escaping hell forever,
separated for all eternity.
As bodies groan in anguish,
descended in a pit so low;
If only on earth they had listened,
but now the truth they know.

# I know you
## Jeremiah 1:5

Ever so gently I adjust the clay;
My chosen one, My beautiful vessel,
I will illuminate your way.
I know all life's decisions,
you will have to make.
But I give you My word,
no more on you, than you can take.

I'm imparting your teardrops;
but just to let you know,
I will store each one in My bottle
as you let them flow.
Tenderly I'll strengthen your heart,
that will shatter and break;
Adding My endurance for your suffering,
this pain you'll be able to take.

## Come to Me

*I'm smiling as I add
the colouring to your skin;
I'm leaving My imprint,
a reflection of Jesus your King.
Each hair I have specially numbered
upon your head;
My gift is My wisdom,
for where your feet will tread.*

*I'm teaching you forgiveness,
to let offenses go;
I see you'll wrestle with this,
My child, I understand and know.
A voice for singing,
I've finely tuned;
My abundance of grace,
to cope with every deep wound.*

*I know you*

*I've given you My hopes,
My dreams and what I've planned;
Promising to hold tight,
I'll never let go of your hand.
I'm adding perseverance to your inner man;
You'll always conquer victoriously,
with Jesus your Lamb.*

*I've made an intimate place,
in your heart for only Me;
My gift is My will,
My freedom to set you free.
I impart in you My divinity,
The Truth and the Light;
I've given you spiritual eyes,
to see with clearer insight.*

## Come to Me

*My* timer is set for when you are due home;
All heaven anticipates your arrival,
around My great throne.
I continually whisper to you,
just to let you know,
My child I know all about you,
oh how I love you so!

# I've Been There
## Isaiah 53

When the pain feels so unbearable,
I'm holding tighter to your hand;
As you stare in disbelief and bewilderment,
I will help you to understand.
I see, you've cried so many tears
and still there's many to flow,
But I want to tell you something very special,
just to let you know.

You see, I've been there,
where there's no words to describe the pain.
Though numb and shocked, I promise to comfort,
strengthen and raise you up again.
I know exactly what you're going through,
I experienced it long ago.
I allowed Myself to feel,
so I would understand and know.

*I've been there when loved ones died
and the pain just swallows you up.
I felt the devastating blow when
I drank from the sinners' cup.
I've felt that emptiness and nothingness
as you try your best to smile.
Please come, rest with Me;
I've been there, stay with Me a while.*

*I've been there when the storms raged
and all looked utterly bleak;
Slumped over in My arms,
you know I carried you so desperately weak.
I know what it's like
when there's no words that can be spoken,
Absolutely devastated and shattered,
but I'll mend those pieces that are broken.*

*You see, I've been there,
I felt every lash that ripped upon My back,
I felt the agonising pain
as the cross slumped across My neck,
I felt that rejection. Oh!
The pain was so painfully deep.
I soothe you, as I cradle you,
calmly gifting you with My sleep.*

*I've been there,
just like you, and your Father sees it all;
I promise you this, you'll recover,
again you'll stand so tall.
I know because I've been there
as I stood completely alone in your place;
I gave My everything and with hatred
they spat upon My face.*

## I've Been There

*I've been there, as the nails were hammered,
in anguish I hung in pain;
I felt it all, I've been there,
as I cried out My Father's Name.
I watched as death hovered over Me,
taunting soon you'll die.
Yes! You see I've been there,
I've experienced it all.
My child, I do understand, when you cry.*

# Jesus
### Revelation 1:12-18

What an amazing,
an incredible and beautiful Man;
The purest Lily of the Valley,
our quiet and peaceful Lamb.
Eternally ageless, a sovereign and mighty King,
Faithful Friend to the fatherless
and in control of everything.

Eyes reflecting like diamonds,
shining ever so bright,
Stands in His own beaming radiance,
surrounded by majestic light.
Gentle steps revealing His sacrifice,
His priceless gift to us all;
Whispering, when He lovingly speaks,
our Rescuer from the fall.

How gracious is our awesome King,
forever holding all power!
Our watchful Guard, hidden Refuge,
a great imposing Tower.
The all-compassionate One,
so caring and completely true;
Endless names He's given
and He gave His life for you.

He's the Alpha and Omega,
covering all span of time;
Wisdom to the fullest,
who would dare Him undermine.
Speechless beauty, perfect Judge,
faithful in all His ways;
Majesty, our Abba Father,
the Ancient of Days.

*Jesus*

*Never-changing, all-knowing One,
fullness of grace—
Kindness and love mirrors marvellously
from His face.
He's the everlasting One,
with such a gracious hand,
Passing throughout life's ages,
forever and ever, His kingdom will stand.*

# The Rescuer Has Come
## Revelation 1:12-18

Securing Himself around you,
fastening Himself ever so tight,
Defences placed on every side,
guarding you with all His might.
The Rescuer has come, a fortified city,
all He will slay;
Cunningly the enemy comes
but He just blows them all away.

A sign "Do Not Trespass"
erected and clearly to be seen,
The Rescuer completely focused
on their every ploy and scheme.
A safe house, guarded royalty,
favour from above—
He's your mighty Rescuer,
defending His sacrificial Love.

No one dare touch you,
His banners are placed on show;
Jealous for your protection,
and this they will surely know:
Your Rescuer has come,
never will He slumber or no moment lost,
Guarding, protecting and shielding you,
at every Kingdom cost.

"Not another step closer",
the Father clearly states,
Defending you from the enemy,
the children satan hates.
The Rescuer has come,
plucking you from the enemy's net.
Jesus laughs out loud,
as He watches the snares they set.

*Heavy chains lie scattered,
each link is broken in two;
Evidence of God's mercy,
when the enemy came for you.
A statement decreed,
"No interfering, this child is Mine",
Take your shame and distress,
you're wasting all your time.*

*He hides you from all danger,
you've no need to be alarmed;
Not one part of your body,
will He allow to be harmed.
A mighty sword now wielded,
resting in the Rescuer's hand;
All enemies now scatter,
not one left to stand.*

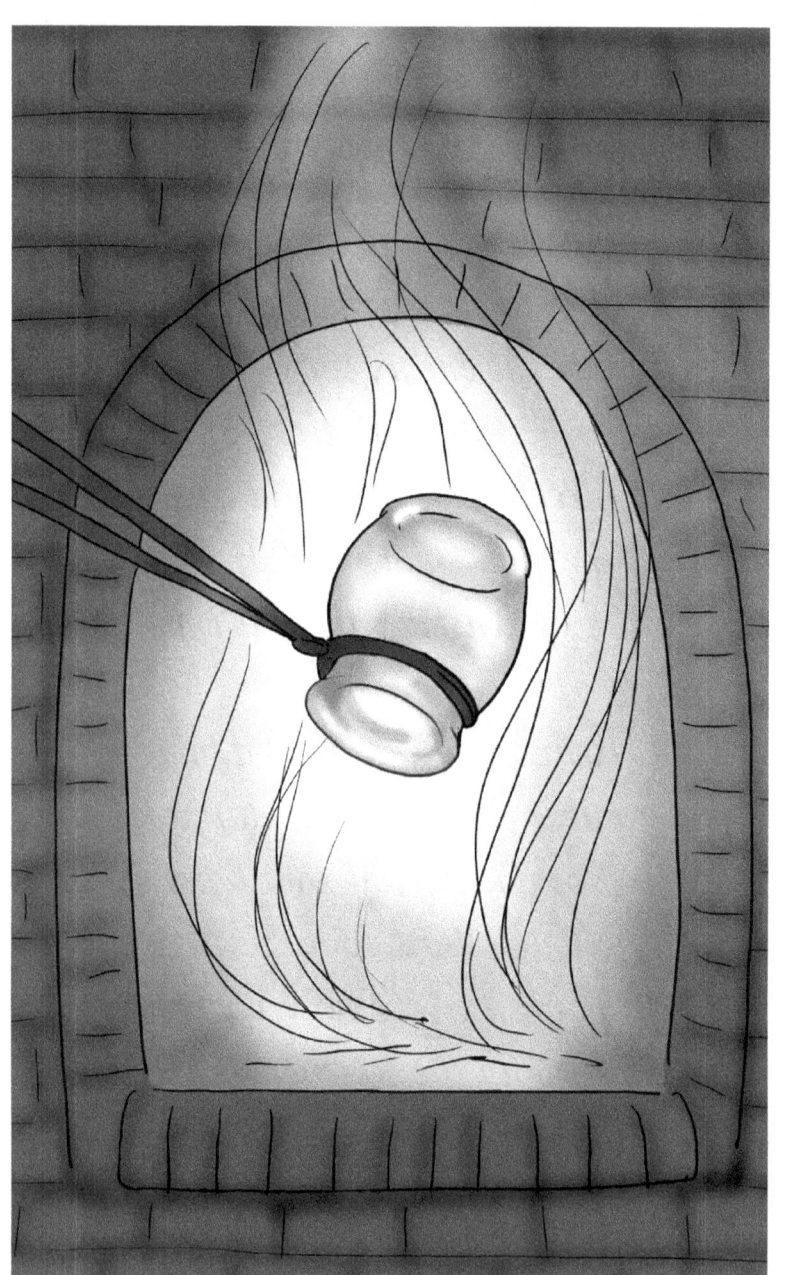

# The Refiner's Fire
## Isaiah 48:10

The Refiner's fire is now ready,
He knows exactly what to do.
Through this refining process,
He will never take His eyes off you.
The Purifier looks lovingly upon
His beloved's heart,
A transforming, a moulding,
a melting He will start.

An enduring heat now works,
as He bends and tempers the will;
His purpose is to purge,
the impurities He desires to kill.
A stirring, an extracting,
the dross He works to skim;
Repeating it over and over,
the process He starts to begin.

## Come to Me

The burning fire separates,
a pouring out will soon take place.
He works until there's no chaff,
no self, not a single trace.
Liked metal forged,
it submits effectively in His hand—
A stretching, a testing,
is what the Refiner's planned,

A struggle, an emptying,
a brokenness through the pain;
Over and over He works,
the flesh He works to tame.
A yielding to surrender,
He ultimately does desire,
As He works for His kingdom,
through the intense refining fire.

*A reflection from a substance,
now rises from the heat—
A holiness, a purity,
now tears through all defeat.
The flame now flickers,
achieving what it had to do;
The Refiner has now accomplished
His greatest work in you.*

# Come Away with Me
## Psalm 116:7

*I am longing for you,
will you come away with Me?
I your Abba Father,
desire and long for your company.
For you, I'm waiting lovingly,
with a smile upon My face,
Knowing soon you're coming to meet,
at our very special place.*

*Oh! Come away with Me,
let Me show you how eagles soar.
I have a storehouse of priceless treasures,
abundantly much, much more.
Come away, My Child,
rest gently upon My chest;
I'm full of goodness, overflowing joy,
I am life's very best.*

## Come to Me

Gently I'll pour My tenderness,
upon you when we meet.
Come away and rest, My child,
by My side I've placed your seat.
I have things I long joyfully,
for only you to see,
My chosen one, My beloved child,
My first priority.

Come away with Me,
I want to teach you how to live;
My refreshing presence and abundance of peace,
to you I want to give.
Let Me take you places,
you never thought you would see;
Our adventure, spending time together—come,
stay close to Me.

*Come away, let's talk,
tell me what you would like to do.
I'm waiting, I'm prepared to move,
all heaven and earth for you.
Yes! Come and rest, lay down,
close by My side;
You'll receive all I Am,
when in Me you abide.*

# You're So Beautiful to Me
## Psalm 69:30

You're My breathless beauty,
with an amazing heart of gold.
I sing over you with adoration,
your future I will always hold.
There's no one like you, you're beautiful,
My one of a kind;
Unique in all your thinking
and you're always on My mind.

Your smile, your laughter and tears,
you're so beautiful to Me.
I know all about you,
I'm the Creator of all you see.
You've a quiet and beautiful spirit,
with a loving heart;
I'm just so crazy about you,
every single part.

## Come to Me

*I've decorated you in My likeness,
you're the apple of My eye.
I collect your tears in My bottle,
storing them up when you cry.
Oh! You're so beautiful to Me,
scars and flaws you may see;
But I quietly whisper lovingly,
you're so beautiful to Me.*

*Your inner beauty is what matters,
it wells up from inside;
I encourage you, be confident,
you've no need to worry or hide.
You're really so beautiful to Me,
others may walk away;
I will always be close, by your side
I will always stay.*

## You're So Beautiful to Me

You're so valued and so special,
a beautiful woman shining through;
I sing over you in awesome wonder,
a special song for you.
You've inner qualities, an amazing character,
a perseverance that will get you through.
Yes! You really are so beautiful
and there's no one just like you!

# In the Shadows
## Psalm 30

Creeping shadows now awake,
as the moonlight arrives
Illuminating the disappointment,
grief and mixed emotions in our lives.
Another sleepless night,
restlessly calls you from your bed,
The King of Light,
watches so closely overhead.

Thinking will it never be normal
or never feel the same,
But watching in the shadows
is an understanding and powerful Name.
Oh! The loneliness, the grief,
only the memories you know;
The Man in the shadows is coming to help
and to comfort you so.

## Come to Me

Night time doesn't tick,
the ticking hand stands still,
Everything's so completely silent,
there's so much time to kill.
A Presence moves in the shadows,
with such a gentle ease,
It moves around to carry,
comfort and do as it will please.

A yearning for daylight,
to desperately breakthrough,
Out from the shadows,
an invisible hand extends to you.
A longing, a desperation,
hours of time to think,
Falling from your heartache,
onto your knees you sink.

## In the Shadows

*Overwhelmed, a deep breath,*
*it's so hard to bear,*
*But the Master's in the shadows,*
*He's always been there.*
*The Encourager,*
*Burden-lifter and an understanding King,*
*Strong to carry this,*
*He'll bring you through this impossible*
*thing.*

*As He steps from the darkness,*
*the shadows expel and disappear.*
*As the breaking of daylight comes,*
*rays of hope begin to appear.*
*Joy comes in the morning,*
*after the exhausting and emotional fight,*
*All along in the shadows was the victorious*
*and conquering Light!*

# Come Soar
## Isaiah 40:31

Come soar to heights and free fall,
through the vastness of space;
Refusing to hold back,
come to this liberated and open place.
You've no need to shelter,
the storm won't touch you here;
Through the driving winds of life,
there's no need to fret or fear.

The mountain peaks are waiting,
for you to come and soar;
The views and scenery like nothing else,
so breathtakingly more.
Come glide like the eagle and leave it all behind;
Refreshment, timeout, a quiet and peaceful mind.

*Come to Me*

Rise above your circumstances,
as you freely let all go.
Come soar to My altitude,
there's no need to look below.
Those who wait upon Me,
will feel completely alive,
Like the eagle soaring from unimaginable
heights, they prepare to dive.

Ascend far above the clouds,
where the atmosphere's so still;
Aim higher, much higher,
come and have your fill.
Yes! I challenge you,
surge higher than ever before;
Mount on eagle's wings,
rise to the skies, come soar.

*I will meet you on the highway,*
*the jet stream in the sky.*
*You will run and not grow weary,*
*spread your wings, come fly.*
*The sun always shines here,*
*all else melts away.*
*Feel the freedom,*
*be released of your burdens this day.*

*Be bold, take courage as you tower*
*above the plain;*
*There's much more climbing*
*and so much height to gain.*
*Come soar, take refuge,*
*take a deep breath of the air—*
*Come soar like the eagles, come if you dare.*

# Never Alone
## Psalm 56:8

The solitude, the isolation,
as the silence lingers on,
I'm whispering in the stillness,
be bold, be courageous, be strong.
You're pretending in the crowd
but at home no one can see;
You're never alone,
I'm calling, bring your loneliness to Me.

I'm a Friend to the fatherless,
I help the lonely to stand,
Placing into families, this is My promise
and what I've planned.
Your beating heart so clearly heard,
the only familiar sound,
It's like you've disappeared and longingly,
want to be found.

## Come to Me

*Overwhelming rejection,
piercing pains within your heart,
Wrestlings overflowing,
as your world just falls apart.
You're never alone,
I will never forsake you, like others do.
From within your loneliness,
I will lift and will carry you.*

*A stepping forward, a facing up,
to another brand-new day;
Loneliness in your heart,
as your painted smile just fades away.
No, it's not My will,
that mankind should ever be alone;
I see your struggle,
but you are never on your own.*

*Disconnected, feeling lost,
as you stand out in the crowd,
Smiling faces laughing,
but still your loneliness shouts out loud.
You're not forgotten, you're never alone,
though it may feel that way—
I'm your greatest Companion,
beside you I will walk each day.*

## CONTACT

If you wish to contact the author, visit
www.SoniaKinning.com

## INSPIRED TO WRITE A BOOK?

Contact
Maurice Wylie Media
Inspirational Christian Publisher

Based in Northern Ireland
and distributing across the world.
www.MauriceWylieMedia.com

www.ingramcontent.com/pod-product-compliance
Lightning Source LLC
Chambersburg PA
CBHW071906070526
44583CB00016B/1870